Ordinary Places, Sacred Spaces

ORDINARY PLACES, SACRED SPACES

Poetry and Prose by Evelyn Mattern
Artwork by Helen David Brancato

BAYEUX

ORDINARY PLACES, SACRED SPACES

© 2005 Evelyn Mattern, Helen David Brancato and Bayeux Arts, Inc.

Published by Bayeux Arts, Inc.

119 Stratton Crescent SW, Calgary, Canada T3H 1T7

www.bayeux.com

Book design by David Lane

Edited by Jennifer Mattern

Library and Archives Canada Cataloguing in Publication—

Mattern, Evelyn

   Ordinary places, sacred spaces / poetry and prose by Evelyn

      Mattern ; artwork by Helen David Brancato.

ISBN 1-896209-59-9

   1. Sacred space--Miscellanea. 2. Spiritual life. I. Brancato, Helen David. II. Title.

PS3563.A858O7 2005   128   C2005-901775-9

First Printing: October 2005

Printed in Canada

The Publisher gratefully acknowledges the financial support of the Canada Council for the Arts, the Alberta Foundation for the Arts, and the Government of Canada through The Book Publishing Industry Development Program.

Books published by Bayeux Arts, under its Bayeux and Gondolier imprints, are available at special quantity discounts to use as premiums and sales promotions, or for use in corporate or organizational training programs. For more information, please write to Special Sales, Bayeux Arts, Inc., 119 Stratton Crescent SW, Calgary, Canada T3II 1T7.

Maison, pan de prairie, ô lumière du soir
Soudain vous acquérez presque une face humaine
Vous êtes près de nous, embrassants, embrassés.

House, patch of meadow, oh evening light
Suddenly you acquire an almost human face
You are very near us, embracing and embraced.

—Rainer Maria Rilke, translated into French by Claude Vigée,
in *Les Lettres*; Source: *The Poetics of Space* by Gaston Bachelard

Late in the kitchen
deep sighs from the weary self
Empathy for all

—Evelyn Mattern, from "Maura 'Soshin' O'Halloran:
Haikus" in *Why Not Become Fire?*

CONTENTS

INTRODUCTION

"Once upon a time in a faraway kingdom" begins many a tale. Time and place are the unconditional settings for a story and for a life. "Redeem the time," sings the poet, but the place may offer the grace that helps to redeem the time and ourselves. Clare of Assisi clasping the altar for sanctuary, Martin Luther King hearing God speak in the kitchen, John Muir striding through the Rockies, Mother Teresa walking the streets of Calcutta, Jacob wrestling with the angel at Bethel, the House of God, the gate of Heaven: who can imagine these spiritual giants without the specific places where they engaged with their destinies?

A life can be told in terms of place. Childhood kitchens and playing fields, schoolrooms and summer camps, boardrooms and bedrooms, hospital rooms and graves. Or, alternatively, refugee camps and mean city streets, prison cells and trenches, killing fields and graves. My own childhood place was urban. I counted thirteen trees in our neighborhood and delighted to grow gourds in our small backyard. In summer, I escaped to my uncle's house near the ocean to exult in the empty beach in late afternoon, the lily pads on the pond of a nearby golf course, and the huge blue spruces enveloping my uncle's home. I would crawl under them to hide from my cousins and read all afternoon.

As an adult, when I've had a choice, I've chosen rural places. A mobile home on an acre in pine woods, for example, where a nearby stream could be followed through several changes of scene. The pines grew on land that undulated with the memory of the furrowed fields of the farm that once thrived at the place. My neighbor's children often found arrowheads in the woods, relics from even earlier days of tribes who hunted under the ancient trees that were felled to make the furrows.

Now I live in another place, in a log cabin on a hill—for me, the *axis mundi* of the world that I return to, as through a labyrinth of traffic and meetings and daily duties. Each night, I pilgrim home to a place of silence, a place where time can seem to stop. Here I grow a few vegetables and lots of flowers in a sunny space that grows smaller each year from the encroaching woods. If I stay here long enough, the oaks and pines and holly trees will embrace the house. The view from the window will be pure green light filtered by the leaves against the windows. The logs of the house may sprout companion leaves to greet the approaching trees. I will not mind too much.

Contemplative places need not be rural, of course. Monasteries tend to be in pastoral settings, but some of the greatest contemplatives live in urban madness. Someone once asked, "Why is a smoke-filled caucus room not perceived as holy as a smoke-filled sanctuary?" The answer is in the eyes of the beholder and the heart of the participants in the caucus. Dag Hammarskjöld, Secretary-General of the UN, carved his contemplative record, *Markings*, out of intensely busy diplomatic days dealing with life and death issues. On airplanes, in conference rooms, in jeeps, he distilled the complexities of his daily life into literary jewels—many of them questions to the universe that hint of deep mystical experience.

SACRED PLACES

Human history can be told in terms of sacred places. Eden—paradise, the garden of our nostalgia and longing—is a primordial holy place. The telling and retelling of its story has fixed in the hearts of hundreds of generations the image of a garden as God's place. Deserts and other wildernesses are also crucial to the human heart. Hebrew prophets, Jesus, and Mohammed all met God in the desert, and many indigenous peoples initiate their youth by sending them into the wilderness.

When Moses approaches the burning bush, God tells him to take off his sandals because he is standing on holy ground. God cares about place. Holy places for Christians include Jerusalem, Rome, Mt. Athos, Canterbury, Campostello, and other pilgrim destinations. Jews travel to pray at the Western Wall, and Muslims seek to visit Mecca at least once in their lives. Buddhists trek to the Bodhi Tree where the Buddha gained enlightenment. Hindus venerate, bathe in, and are consigned at death to the Ganges. All of nature is sacred to the Native American, but kivas, sweat lodges, and burial mounds hold special significance. Stone circles like Stonehenge manifested the divine for primitive peoples. The Greeks had sacred groves.

Place has power. For primitive peoples, sacred places set apart from everyday life—caves, stone circles, grottoes, woods—exercised control over the rest of life. The medieval cathedral rose from a commanding space at the center of the town. Major community decisions are made in the kivas of the Pueblo peoples. The Psalms exhort Jews to turn to Jerusalem as a refuge, and indeed three major religions claim Jerusalem as a holy place. As children in Catholic school, we were encouraged to build May altars at home, placing flowers before a statue of the Madonna every day in May. Meditation teachers in every tradition encourage their students to set aside a special place, even a closet, for meditation, marking off that space with a curtain or an icon or a lighted candle.

Some historians of religion make the point that the Judaeo-Christian tradition emphasizes time over space. Abraham Heschel notes that holiness in space, in nature, was known in other religions, but Judaism shifted the emphasis from space to time, from the realm of nature to the realm of history or events. "The day of the Lord," he says, is more important to the prophets than "the house of the Lord." In Judaism and Christianity runs the line of thought that there are no inherently holy places because God is not bound to one place.

On the other hand, one might say that since God is everywhere, all places are holy, especially when consecrated by human acts that imitate divine love and justice. A church or a kitchen can also be blessed by the prayers said there, by the caring rituals performed there. A pond or a prison cell or a hospital bed can be a place for meeting the present God or the absent God. During the war in El Salvador in the 1980s, I heard many people say, "The martyrs make the space for us to act." The faith-filled survivors understood that righteous ac-

tion requires an amplitude for the gesture of a good person at the right moment. Holiness enters into the "here" as well as the "now."

SPIRITUAL GEOGRAPHY

We use the language of place to describe states of being in the world. "Sanctuary" can be a physical place or an inner refuge. The "desert" represents a literal or a figurative emptiness that seekers flee to or from. We desire to "dwell" or be "rooted" in God, whom the Psalms often image as "shelter," and we speak of the "in-dwelling" of the Holy Spirit. Humility is "knowing one's place." We look for "grounding" in God, and to some, God is indeed the "Ground of being." We walk a spiritual "path," or the "way" of Buddha, or the Tao (Way). Jesus too calls himself "the Way," and the incarnation or birth of Jesus connotes that God becomes human in a concrete place at a specific time. So important is place to the soul that the Rule of St. Benedict mandates a vow of stability whereby monks and nuns commit themselves to a place for life.

In *Day of a Stranger*, Thomas Merton points to particular places near the monastery that are part of his spiritual geography: "Here is the place on the path where I killed a copperhead. There is the place where I saw the fox run daintily and carefully for cover carrying a rabbit in his mouth. And there is the cement cross that, for no reason, the novices rescued from the corner of a destroyed wall and put up in the woods."

These places were hallowed for him by their connection with his story. We also know from his striking photographs and attentive drawings of wagon wheels, weeds, seed pods, and old millstones he found on the monastery property that Merton regarded with reverence the simple, natural objects of his place.

Who among us does not have a catalog of places that tell our story and that we hope to share with those who come after us? "There is the house your great-grandparents lived in. In the back was a kitchen where my grandmother worked twelve hours a day at the end of summer, cooking and canning tomatoes from the garden that was then back there, by that falling-down fence. In summer, we slept on the porch upstairs, and your great-aunt Silvia and I would stay up all night telling stories. Sometimes, we'd climb down the drainpipe and run to the creek." We describe these places with love and nostalgia. They have been sanctified by the rituals of our childhood.

LOSS OF PLACE

Contemporary commerce and technology foster a loss of a sense of place. Modern architect LeCorbusier called a house "a machine to live in." Jobs and aspirations lead Americans in particular to change houses numerous times in the course of our lives. Public spaces like malls and airports are everywhere the same, and identical clothing and refreshments can be bought in Every County, USA. In Rome, I visited a McDonald's sumptuous with fountains, statuary, and Italian gelato, but the main fare was nonetheless standard-issue fries and burgers. I did not eat.

In the southern United States, where I live, building and so-called development hurtle forward, leveling farms and thick woods for concrete highways. Ironically, new banks and office buildings resembling temples reach skyward on choice downtown sites, while new churches in suburban neighborhoods blend in with the landscape or houses there. As everywhere becomes the same and easily accessible, does anywhere become more important? As the sacred and the secular blur, what distinguishes one place from another? How crucial is it to our human and divine identities that any such distinctions remain possible?

Mircea Eliade says that the religious person's nostalgia is to inhabit a divine world: our desire is that our house shall be like the house of the gods.

Even a profane world carries traces of a "religious valorization" of the world. We desire to create a home, a hearth, a safe and beautiful place, a point of orientation toward the rest of our life and the world. Primitive peoples built their houses at the *axis mundi*—the center of the world. We long to go forth into the world from a center, and from a centered place in ourselves. The agony of homelessness has to do with the loss of more than physical shelter. To have no home is to lack not only a roof and four walls; it is to lack an orientation or place in society. It is to have no place in the world.

In broader terms, religious ecologists describe a "cosmic homelessness" afflicting humankind, particularly in the West, that prompts a lack of care for the earth. Christians who have accepted too literally the idea that this world is not our home, that mere temporal space does not matter, have an unconcern that leads to wanton disregard of the health and welfare of our planet, the only home we have known. Augustine says, "Thou has made us for Thyself, O Lord, and our hearts are restless till they rest in thee." We needn't deny that restlessness that makes us desire to rest only in God, but we might recognize that the cosmos itself is restless. According to theologian John Haught, we are on "a long pilgrimage not *from* the universe but *with* the universe."

As the center of time is "now," the center of space is "here," but contemporary physics tells us neither is a point. Alfred North Whitehead affirms, "In a certain sense, everything is everywhere at all times. For every location involves an aspect of itself in every other location. Thus every spatio-temporal standpoint mirrors the world." It mirrors the divine as well. Truly the earth is our place of grace, and every place upon it can be a sacrament.

SACRAMENT

Sacrament is what reveals the divine. Before the twelfth century and the determination of the present list of seven sacraments in the Roman Catholic tradition, the term "sacrament" had the broader meaning of any manifestation of God in time and space. It also conveyed a sense of hiddenness or mystery. In subsequent centuries, the sacraments were seen as marking the times of a person's life, and they used the basic stuff of the earth: bread from the kitchen, wine from the vine, oil from the tree, and water from the stream.

Places have also been graced by blessings and sacramentals, concrete symbols of the holy. Labyrinths, holy water fonts, incense, relics, blessed palm, icons, candles, and statues have long been found in churches and homes. The Protestant Reformation discarded many of these objects, but some have made their way back into contemporary churches— testimony to the human need for sensible reminders of God. Buddhists use bells, incense, candles, statues, and flowers. For Native Americans, corn, sage bundles, feathers, the drum, and the dance are holy. They mark places as well as occasions. They remind us that in addition to "the sacrament of the present moment," we can attend to "the sacrament of the present place." Here and now are both occasions of grace.

Eliade says that the religious person thirsts for being, and where the sacred manifests itself in space, the real unveils itself—and the world comes into existence. Though not overtly religious, Henry David Thoreau went off to the woods in search of the real. "I wished to live deliberately, to front only the essential facts of life, and see if I could not learn what it had to teach, and not, when I came to die, discover that I had not lived." Walden was for him a holy place. Its trees were shrines; its ponds in their transparency were more beautiful than many human lives. He sought out not mountaintops nor cathedrals but an ordinary pond and the woods just a few miles outside of Concord. Like Jesus, who spent most of his time on footpaths, in fragile boats, at tables for meals.

This book speaks to and visualizes the sacred in the ordinary, the holy in this place, the here as well as now. Artist and writer have chosen to be attentive to certain ordinary places made holy by who comes there and what happens there. Sometimes it takes an artist to show the reality we are swimming in. Sometimes the artist has to be taught by the images that arrive. Only after we—artist and writer— had assembled a list of places we knew to be holy, did we realize that many of them are liminal places. Thresholds, borders, beaches, porches, refugee camps, nursing homes—these are places in between life and death, neither in nor out, touching both sky and sea, old and new, day and night, sleep and waking, being and non-being. Such places heighten our awareness of our lives suspended between heaven and earth. Feet rooted in an earthy home, our head and hands probe a reality we seek to pry open with attention. Given our attention, everywhere is grace. *Given our attention.*

THRESHOLDS

Beside my front door hangs an arresting woodcut of the doorway that Austrian farmer Franz Jaegerstaetter walked through on his way to be beheaded for refusing to fight in Hitler's army. The woodcut, called "The Door to the Road Taken," shows the front door of Jaegerstaetter's house from the inside. A dark hallway surrounds the door frame, which opens onto a brighter outdoor space with a tree near its center standing next to a road that curves into the distance. Without knowing the woodcut's story, nearly everyone who visits me comments on it. No doubt that's because artist Robert McGovern has captured a sense of both transition and transcendence, elements that make the doorway a symbol of passage. I hung the picture next to my front door to remind myself whenever I leave home that each passage may be my last and should have purpose.

Doorways and windows have always been intriguing portals for me. Usually I stand outside looking in, curious about what the lives inside are like. Skittish about being thought a peeping Thomasina, I nevertheless peer sideways into lighted windows at dusk and walk my dog through neigh-

My midnight window frames ebony / until the stars puncture the sky / and the moon, half full or more, lightens / the aisles between the winter trees.

borhoods with lovely gardens that offer clues about their gardeners' lives. I most enjoy passing houses in Central America where the doorway on the street opens into a cool courtyard with wooden chairs and hammocks shaded by plants. Fascinating are the hints they give about family and relationships. Doorways are thresholds that give glimpses into the lives of others.

> Glancing into courtyards
> behind the open doors of Latin houses,
> I spy lush gardens
> and grandmothers rocking
> in carved teak chairs
> as babies crawl in the home's heart.

> Traffic on the street
> compels my ear but not my eye.
> Do the grandmothers see
> this traveler at the door
> with open sky behind her,
> backpack her only burden?

In some cultures, one bows, prostrates, or touches the hand to the doorway in passing. Doorways or gates are traditional places of sacrifice and judgment. Jacob wrestled with the angel at "the gate of Heaven," and the Gospel admonishes us to "enter by the narrow gate." Jews attach a mezuzah to the door post, and Catholics place a holy water font nearby. Windows hold similar spiritual significance. They speak of possibility, penetration, and consciousness. Paintings of the Annunciation of the angel to Mary often feature a window, a doorway, or a portico symbolizing the coming of the divine into our human space. At the basilica in Assisi, Viterbo's *Annunciation* shows Mary sitting on a porch and the angel spanning two windows opening into a starry night sky. Grace is flowing both ways!

Thresholds of all kinds lie between two modes of being, inside and outside, past and future, sleeping and waking, conscious and unconscious, sacred and profane. The prime liminal moment is the one between sleeping and waking, a time that artists prefer for the access it gives to the unconscious.

Thomas Merton understood dawn to be this *point vierge*, the threshold between darkness and light, between being and nonbeing. He noted carefully the woods and birds at dawn when creation in its innocence asks permission "to be" once again. For humans, the *point vierge* is the nothingness at our center that belongs entirely to God.

I live surrounded by woods and sleep near a large double window framing a darkness that usually shows some light from moon or stars. In the night, I wake to total silence and the pregnant woods beyond the window. Or do I wake? Perhaps I am still dreaming in the elemental presence of the woods and the quiet.

My midnight window frames ebony
until the stars puncture the sky
and the moon, half full or more, lightens
the aisles between the winter trees.

Falling to sleep in the dark, I hear
only stirrings from the dog's dream,
the hum of the refrigerator,
and green wood crackling in the stove.

Meanwhile the snow flings its flimsy veil
across the land, and the veil clings
till day. In the light, I see the tracks
deep and cloven from the night deer,

syllabary from the birds' fingers,
and ovals brushed by belly hair
of the low-slung foxes on their way.
Some other tracks I do not know,

but what I can name says enough.
The dark beyond our sleeping
is full beyond our knowing
and not the emptiness we think.

KITCHENS

In earlier times in the West, as in some parts of the world today, the heart of the household was the hearth. In Latin, the word for hearth means "focus." Here, food was prepared, and members of the household gathered to keep warm by the fire.

Kitchens are today's hearths, generating warmth even where cooking is done in microwaves and convection ovens. Even in the era of TV and fractured family schedules, kitchens remain gathering places for family. Thanksgiving, our national holy day that transcends religious differences and is for many scattered families the only time they come together, centers on the feast from the kitchen.

Our kitchen when I was a child was the place where we ate everyday meals amid heated discussion about sports, politics, and religion. At the big wooden table we also played board games, worked on jigsaw puzzles, and did our homework, reciting memorized social-studies paragraphs to our mother while she cooked. Mornings, mother forbade us to come downstairs until she had her ritual coffee, sitting at the kitchen table in the quiet. My father gone to work, she wanted only the cat for company

Mornings, mother forbade us to come downstairs

until she had her ritual coffee,

sitting at the kitchen table in the quiet.

in that early morning hour. I sometimes perform the same coffee ritual.

Kitchens are obvious contemplative places. So many rhythmic and repetitive actions keep them humming: peeling potatoes, cutting up and grating vegetables, stirring sauces and soups, kneading bread, making coffee, washing dishes, feeding cats and dogs. These actions offer meditative possibilities, breathing moments in the midst of a hectic day. In many Central American villages, where the kitchen is usually a structure set off from the house to keep it cooler, women sit to grind corn at *metates*, curved stones that look exactly like the pre-Colombian ones in museums. The ritual of the grinding can go on for hours, as it has gone on for thousands of years. It is mesmerizing to watch and to do.

"Dura y suelta"
the old one says
as she rolls the thousand-year-old stone
across the dough.

"Dura y suelta"
the old one is:
flesh like ripe olives,
eyes in canyons cut from the earth's
original face.

Inviting someone into your kitchen and sharing the fruits of your kitchen are consummate acts of hospitality, which is at the heart of most religions. Formal guests don't usually get invited into the kitchen. We share our kitchens with our intimates. Meals are also for sharing. Fresh coffee sits beside heads put together in sympathy and understanding. Making bread is more than a meditative art; the gift of a homemade loaf is among the most thoughtful. It's an extension of Eucharist.

Or perhaps Eucharist is an extension of the gift of homemade bread. When Jesus sent his disciples to secure the Upper Room for the Last Supper, he must have known that a kitchen was included in the contract. As Jesus and the twelve reclined at table to share these last, sacred intimacies, the women disciples were preparing food nearby and carrying it to the table. They made the bread, blessed it before it was blessed by the Lord, and—with this Lord—no doubt shared in the meal and the bread. In one sense, every time we share a meal, we share Eucharist.

Saint Catherine of Siena knew this truth. Legend has it that this "people's saint," after she died, stopped by a friend's house in Rome to prepare a meal for the family before her soul went on to heaven.

> The door of the dream
> where we usher out the day,
> invites us into the night's
> dark mine, into the manger's
> pressed well of hay
> where we may lie down,
> may lay down ourselves.

> The path beyond the door
> is not well worn.

> Too little have we gone
> over to the neighbor's side,
> too little sat in the bright
> room that smells of fresh
> coffee and rising bread.

> Open the door to the poor
> donkey who brays
> from its hobbled soul.
> Lead it back across
> the sleepy threshold,
> unbind with tending hand
> patient with the mind's knots.

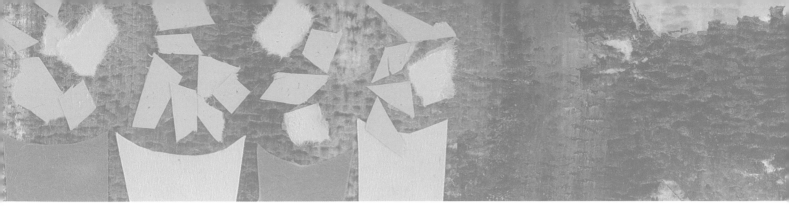

PORCHES

Despite what the thesaurus says, a *porch* is not a *verandah*, is not a *piazza*, is not a *solarium* or *gallery* or *lanai* or *levee*. A porch has a homeliness about it that these supposed synonyms fail to convey. True, all these names describe an open-air but roofed structure with walls on no more than one or two sides. All are open to the outdoors yet sheltered, clasped in one arm of the mother house if you will, her apron held over the child's head for protection from the rain. But a porch is for shelling peas. A gallery is not. One might drink a mint julep on a verandah, but beer seems more fitting for a porch.

Even a church porch is a homely place, according to seventeenth-century poet George Herbert. His poem "The Church Porch" introduces a book of elegant metaphysical poems called *The Temple*. Most of the poems in the book are dialogues between a soul and God, both psychologically complex and theologically profound. The transcendent final poem, "Love," inspired philosopher Simone Weil. "The Church Porch," on the other hand, is a versified set of didactic counsels against gambling

Under the heat I followed him slowly home

along the new government sewer

to his porch of marigolds in coffee cans

morning glories strung up from buckets

petunias in jars.

and drinking, and a series of exhortations to living simply, dressing appropriately, and kneeling for prayer. Such is the stuff of porch conversations, even at church.

A porch is a threshold to a house, but it acts more like an escape from a house's heat and complexities. Those of us who grew up in cities understand that porches on "row houses" are places to retreat to on hot summer evenings. On a good day, you can watch from the porch how the rain hits the asphalt, and you feel the temperature fall in minutes. In the evening, a child can inch her way down the front steps without being noticed and scoot up the street to play Red Rover with her friends. Any passerby hears on the porches murmurs of a dozen conversations at once, children whispering, adults telling stories or comparing notes on where to buy tires or tomatoes or deciding whether to attempt a family vacation this year. When I moved to the South, I realized that the elegant wraparound porches of traditional Southern white frame houses play the same role as the relatively cramped city porches of my childhood. The tea might be sweeter, but the conversations and confidences are similar.

Porches foster communion. On a winter night, after the last household task, the last phone call, the last bit of catch-up reading, I go out to my porch to observe the moon in its movements across the sky. It never bores, appearing or not appearing, half hidden beyond the tallest winter branches, often lighting the sky brighter than any searchlight in the city twenty miles away. Sitting on a shady porch on a hot and humid afternoon and staring out at the trees lulls a person, as Andrew Marvell says, "annihilating all that's made to a green thought in a green shade."

Porches also nurture self-expression. Those who can't afford fancy flower pots, elegant trellises, and outdoor furniture find that painted kitchen chairs and ancient rockers do very well. Some of the poorest neighborhoods in the North and South have some of the prettiest, most flower-decked and vine-covered porches. They are places in the sun, places in the shadows, where we can dream what seems impossible indoors.

> In Texas sun
> I saw an old black man
> hatted and gaunt
> retired chairman of no board
> in long-sleeved white starched shirt
> buy fifty cents of New York cheddar in a
>   wine shop.
> "That's the best cheese in the world."

> Under the heat I followed him slowly
>   home
> along the new government sewer
> to his porch of marigolds in coffee cans
> morning glories strung up from buckets
> petunias in jars.

He at his door,
a pure and brilliant canvas
in an antique wooden frame.

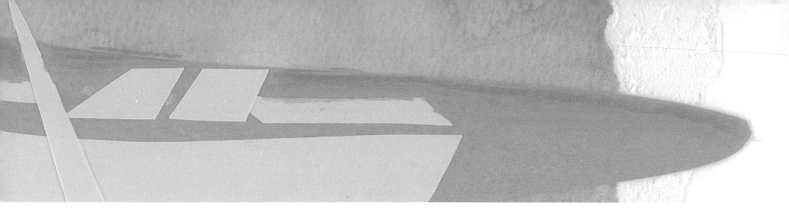

PONDS

Ponds are both source and symbol of life. They foster microscopic forms like algae, and amphibians return there to propagate. Night near a pond vibrates with the sounds of the smallest creatures singing for their lives. Farm ponds provide irrigation for crops, and in Japanese gardening, ponds are vital representations of the sea. Their design is meant to nurture and give strength to the viewer, to reaffirm connections to the earth, and to give courage for the journey. In *Walden*, Henry David Thoreau calls a pond "a field of water" that responds, like long grasses, to the spirit or breath of the air, continually receiving new life and motion from above.

I live near ponds where ducks, beaver, green herons, and great blue herons live. These ponds remind me of both the necessity and the grace in nature. Deer come to drink there every day, and Canada geese arrive in season, prepared to frolic on the water and to give birth to the next generation. The beaver, constructing dams that purify the water, take a break to swim and flap their tails when they sense that they are observed. When I first moved into my house, I opened the back door at dusk to

A pond,
both thresold
and mirror,
lies between
earth and the
heavens and
takes on the
color of both.

find a great blue heron looking in the back window. I wondered as it opened its wings to their full six-foot span and flew off. It has never come so close again, but I feel we have a relationship. It throws off its camouflage on a dead tree trunk and lets out a fractious squawk as I draw near to it on my walks.

A pond, both threshold and mirror, lies between earth and the heavens and takes on the color of both. Unlike the ocean or a large and lapping lake, ponds are smooth mirrors, reflecting pools for the sky and surrounding vistas. Still water, they invite us to sit still beside them and contemplate, not ourselves, like Narcissus, but the strangely beautiful upside-down world where trees hang by their roots, or skyscrapers, by their ground-floor lobbies and parking garages.

See this dependent world: look first at
the pond birds flying underneath us,
wings rippling in the floating sky;
then at the shell-shaped island
hanging by its knees in the center,
a slightly cupped palm for cattails,
willows beginning, grasses, and
cowbird feathers caught on dead
    branches.

Finally, when you have noted well
the old rowboat beached at the edge,
its waterproof companion pointed
    towards the underworld,
pure and fitting craft for the journey,
lose yourself at last in the sky
    underneath,
its very existence attending upon
your refusal to stick your foot in it.

Thoreau also calls ponds "lakes of light" and chose to live by one. He thought Walden Pond his landscape's most expressive feature, the "earth's eye" into which the beholder could look to measure the depth of his or her own nature. Ponds are, according to him, more beautiful than our lives, more transparent than our characters.

There is a small pond at Wellspring, the Church of the Savior's Maryland retreat. Tucked into the trees, the pond remains cool, dark, and quiet on a warm day. It's called Merton Pond, and I have to think it was named for the monk Thomas Merton.

MERTON POND AT WELLSPRING

long pool hiding
    in the shadowy trees
water lilies gazing
    at a blank rock
monk frog plunking
    his complaint to the world

CITY PARKS

Recently I looked out from the top of the tallest building in a nearby city and was struck by the relief, in color and shape, provided by the trees in the landscape. Without them, the bird's eye view would be a canvas of rectangular roofs and parking lots. As it is, trees dot the streets, and clusters here and there signal the presence of parks. Parks are green daubs on a gray canvas.

If it is hot, the park feels cooler. If the streets are slushy from snow, in parks the white beauty lasts longer. If the sky is barely visible among tall buildings, in the park we can see the blue. In parks, the music of calliopes and merry-go-rounds, the jingle bells of ice cream vendors, the calls of children, the chants of demonstrators, and the guitars of street musicians modulate the city's unrelenting rhythms. Unlike the blur of noise that accompanies our dashes between buildings, in parks we allow specific sounds to penetrate our consciousness.

In our country, parks remain one of the few places where many kinds of people come together in a public space. The poor, who have no money to spend, are not invited into suburban malls. In a city park at noon on a weekday, on the other hand, the

gifts and problems of all become evident. Men and women in expensive suits stride along while talking on cell phones. Families and workers eat sandwiches from picnic baskets or hot dogs and falafel bought from vendors. Children play. Old people out for air or some human contact stop to rest on benches. Homeless people sit or sleep, taking rest for their journeys.

Parks also echo the *agora*, the public square at the center of Greek life. The Greeks considered it a sacred space because the discussions that fueled their democracy took place there. According to Juan Edmundo Cirlot, any precinct, enclosure, walled garden, square, park, or castle corresponds to the *temenos*, a sacred and circumscribed space kept guarded because it constitutes a spiritual entity. For us, compartmentalized as we are by race, class, and a host of economic and cultural dividers, any space where we can all be together in relative harmony constitutes a sacred space.

The March wind swathes our cheeks
in cold; the dog outruns her ball.
False spring has blasted the peach
and withered the mouths of daffodils.

The silence of trees opens a space
for reluctant thought to start.
A toothless woman, middle-aged,
stares from behind her cart

of clothes and sacks. Nor is there bench
out of range of a beggar's plea.
Those who yet add land to land
insure we will have the hungry

Narrow men slip among
narrow buildings that steer the wind.
Their narrow leather bags enclose
papers for interests they defend.

Both leather bags and paper sacks
hold all their bearers possess
under leafless trees extending limbs
like the arms of a narrow cross.

In medieval Europe, a sacred space would have been the church, a sacred enclosure at the center of the town where people from all walks of life felt free to enter at any time to rest or pray. It was a cool (or a warm) place set off from the hustle and bustle of the streets outside. Today, if churches have remained in the city, they are likely to be locked, or people from a variety of religious affiliations—or none—don't think of entering them. A park is, in contrast, usually open to everyone. It is not paradise, because we are reminded in a park of the disparities among us. It is a garden, nevertheless, a place for thought and a remembrance of the original garden from which we came and to which we shall return.

Saint Bernard says that monks need a cleared space to encounter the living God. There is a bit of the monk in us all. Though most of us are tied to schedules and places that pull us in too many directions at once, in cities we are drawn to parks as part of our inner and often unrecognized desire to experience the divine aspect that is clarity and peace and a break with routine.

SAILBOATS & BEACHES

Sailboats rock like cradles on the universal sea. They are wombs bearing within them life that is ever sailing, ever evolving, ever changing. Miniature worlds, boats hold only the basic stuff of life: a place to stand, a place to rest, enough food and water till the next port, logs and instruments for guidance. Boats are propelled by wind, the breath of God. Without breath, without spirit, they do not move.

I once spent a week on a friend's boat. A priest who had taken a year off to refurbish a wooden craft that hauled cargo between Florida and the Bahamas, he offered it to me for a retreat. On that boat, I understood his love of silence. It held enough adventure. I never left the dock except in a tiny dinghy I rowed through the marshes in the afternoons, but the deck of the sailboat that suspended me between sky and water was sufficient meditation hall. And the meticulous space below, with its diminutive stove and head, bookshelf and sleeping bench, offered all a body and a soul might need.

Sailboats
rock like
cradles
on the
universal
sea.

ON THE CREDENCE

In this marina ropes make parable:
they tie us faithful up to dock and piling,
protect as netting, hold the hatches
open to our spaces underneath,
hoist our sails as halyards, are
lifeline and preventer to our pride.

New rope moves stiff. Half used, it frets.
Aged, it frays.
As people we are ropes of sand,
in crucial moments separate.
On our high ropes we lose the knack
for telling when it's safe to slip the cable.

Aboard this boat that pulses gently with
     the wind,
I breathe damp ropes of air
cabled to an anchor just outside myself,
close enough for one lone soul to haul,
deep enough to outlast several tides.

Like boats, beaches are places of passage, neither sea nor land, both land and sea. They invite us to change our perspective, expand our view, alter our practice. People who never take off their shoes at home, indoors or outdoors, go barefoot at the beach. Serious adults build castles in the sand, commune with pelicans, speak to strangers on the strand. A friend says he wishes he could keep his "beach mind" all year long. It's like Zen mind, beginner's mind, life in the moment, under the sun or rain, soaking up whatever the beach offers.

Albert Camus, born in Algeria on the Mediterranean, writes lyrically, "Every summer morning on the beach feels like the first morning of the world, and every evening like its solemn ending . . . These are nuptials that can never be forgotten." On the beach, we do feel married to the sky and sea, in communion with surf fishers in cold November, at one with seagulls and the passing porpoises. In contrast, our daily lives in cities and suburbs can feel like divorce, fragmentation, separation from nature, others, and ourselves.

A Greek friend writes about her native island, "I love the sea, with its sensuality and anger, and I love the islanders with the proud foreheads and the rough faces softened by the waves and the south winds. There is something tragic about the ships always coming and going, their expectations for the mercy of the sea." She dwells with her islanders beyond the romanticism of the summer visitor to the beach. Those who live by the sea and depend on it for livelihood know a deeper life. They comprehend the dangers as well as the mercies of the sea. When they choose one, they choose the other, knowingly.

AT CHICAMACOMICO BANKS

Off Hatteras a humpback whale
struggled in calm waters
while her mother watched.

A mile and a half out
two rescue crews paddled
rubber rafts at her side.

Once she brushed her head against
the boat, let a man free her face
with his bare hands. Another

put on a snorkel and went
under, saw abrasions, lines
still wrapping the flukes.

She swam right beneath the boat
and the whales headed south again.
The rescuers, cold and wet,

caught in the net of memory
stood on the beach for hours
before they went home to sleep

They dreamed of swimming in space
and rounding up soft moons.

PLANES, TRAINS & BUSES

Life is a journey, and many heroes travel in order to remind us of that truth. With names like Ulysses, Galahad, Quixote, they are restless, they aspire. They engage in quests for holy grails or go on pilgrimages to holy places. To journey is to seek, and the road or the route is the way of the seeker. Teresa of Avila says that life is a night spent in an uncomfortable inn. Life is also a night ride on a train blowing its lonely whistle at all the sleeping towns along its route. African-American spirituals feature "gospel trains," and Bob Marley sings, "Zion train is coming our way."

Planes, trains, and buses—like other in-between spaces—are venues for possibility. In them we speak more freely with strangers and share intimate stories we hesitate to tell our neighbors at home. Like the pilgrims in *The Canterbury Tales*, we reveal ourselves to those with whom we share the journey. If we are traveling alone, we allow our minds to roam. When I was in graduate school, I took the Paoli Local on the Philadelphia Main Line every day. If I had a seat, my dutiful self would choose to read or study, but failing to get a seat gave me an excuse to sway with all the other standing passengers and let my mind rest, wander, pray.

The Korean man born in Japan
who runs the Italian food stand
at 30th Street Station
smiles as I watch him make
a perfect hoagie for two college girls.

My turn. He wonders if
I'm from New York. I say,
Philadelphia, live in Carolina.
He says he had a girlfriend there.
He thrived in Manhattan,
doesn't like it here.

He lays on carefully the fine sliced
cheese, shredded lettuce, roasted pep-
    pers.
Do I want the onions? Evenly distributed.
The house sauce? Who could refuse it,
offered with his smile? Finally, the tuna.
Few vegetarians in his view.

I hand him bills and change, and he
cups my whole hand in his larger one,
holds it long and hard, cup around cup
around the coins for a meal
to eat later as the train slides
through Virginia in the night.

Now that I am graying,
though less gray than he,
I don't withdraw my hand
Who can grasp the hollow spaces
that well up on a winter afternoon
when a man no longer knows a girl
he might have loved in Carolina?

Planes, trains, and buses offer an alternative visions. On buses, we are likely to rub shoulders with poor people, the ones not mentioned in the guidebooks. From the train, we see the back doors of homes and businesses, a more haphazard and leveling view than from the front. Viewed from the sky, the city at night is an array of jewels, the countryside by day a patchwork quilt of field and forest. My missionary friends had told me that, although the people were lovely, Honduras was a poor and pitiful place. They failed to prepare me for the sheer physical beauty of the country as I approached it for the first time in a plane flying low over steep green mountains and lush valleys.

Just as pilgrimage is a time set apart, planes, trains, and buses are places set apart. They offer space between the goals of our leaving and arriving, between the times of our commitments back there and our responsibilities up ahead. They allow moments to reflect on what has gone before and what is to come. We have left behind a complex of relationships, a job well done, our household mess. We are on our way to introduce our new child to its grandparents, to bury a father or mother, to tackle a new project, to climb a mountain in the Andes. We ride at the juncture of opportunity and risk, the point between dream and responsibility.

Pascua en la tarde
we said goodbye in Michoacan,
Zacatecas, San Luis Potosi,
and Durango
and boarded the big bus.
In three days and two nights,
we stopped three times for a half hour
to buy food and find a bathroom.
At Laredo the *piratas* came on the bus
to change our *pesos* to dollars.

First we talked about what we had left:
our wives and children, half-built houses,
land untilled for lack of money to buy
     seed,
pueblos with no more jobs,
jobs that had moved to the border.

Then we fell silent.

At dawn on the third day,
ten busloads by then, we pulled into
a parking lot in *Carolina del Norte*.

In the warehouse,
we stood to see a video on pesticides.
We paid five dollars for a tortilla break-
    fast with beer
and used the outhouses on the lot.
A man called out the names of *padrones*
and how many workers each would use.

Four hours later
we boarded the buses again
to meet the *padrones*
who use our shoulders for the jobs
people here won't do.

If we keep away from accidents and
    pesticides,
if there is enough rain and the *padron*

does not fail to pay,
if we are not robbed,
we will be in Mexico for Christmas.
Until next Easter
when the buses come again.

NURSING HOMES

In the West, we expect to live long lives. Many of us know at least one person who is a hundred years old and quite a few others in their eighties and nineties. Unfortunately, our society enables quantity of years but not necessarily quality of life. Alzheimer's and other diseases plague the old and make it impossible for families to care for their elders at home. As a result, many middle-aged and even older persons make regular visits to aged relatives in nursing homes. Parents and grandparents ourselves, we may find ourselves needing to be parents to our own parents.

Nursing homes invite us across a threshold that opens onto the last journey we all will make. Their inhabitants are merely farther along on the journey than we are. They have unreeled most of the thread of their life stories, some of them remarkable stories, though quickly forgotten when they no longer entertain in their telling. Nursing home residents' bodies bear the wounds of their work and the twisted limbs of their suffering. Occasional smiles give glimmers of the joy they have known. Sometimes, another life already seems to glow beneath their diaphanous skin.

We wonder what it will feel like when we come to live in these places. Who has heard the words of Jesus to Peter and not been haunted by them? "When you were young you fastened your belt about you and walked where you chose; but when you are old you will stretch out your arms, and a stranger will bind you fast, and carry you where you have no wish to go." When we are thus bound, will we feel the indignity of being spoken to as though we were children? Will we be able to accept being forgotten for who we were and what we achieved? Will we want our framed degrees on the wall, photos of our children and pets on the sill? To remind others of who we were, who we are? To remind ourselves? Will we have enough memory even to care?

Those who work in nursing homes are usually paid little and thanked less. We know that such places, where some have power over others, are fertile ground for abuse, but we know also that some aides and administrators daily transcend themselves and their environment to bring respect and compassion to the fragile ones in their care. They are the hidden servants taking care of the hidden elders. They are among the just ones who keep the world from destruction.

One day I entered the room of a friend's mother and found pasted to her closet a note that testified to a daughter's love and an aide's sensitivity. I realized that this small room shared by two formerly independent women who used to manage households and families—an institutional setting despite the silk flowers, a place smelling of antiseptic and the odors it is meant to camouflage—is a holy place. It is being sanctified by rituals built on respect for the image of God in persons, even when that image seems flickering and unfamiliar.

> MORNING AIDE:
> PLEASE REMEMBER
> RUTH'S UPPER DENTURES.
> RUTH WEARS JEWELRY
> EVERY DAY.
> RUTH WEARS ROUGE
> EVERY DAY.

PLEASE DO NOT PUT HER SOILED
BLANKETS IN THE LAUNDRY.
GIVE THEM TO ME.
    —RUTH'S DAUGHTER

This sign is just to say
Ruth once memorized a face
as I do yours, traced
with her index finger the whorl of an ear
while the refrigerator hummed
against the silence, stroked
the cat into electricity
on a cool blue day.

After her husband died,
she packed daily lunches for her children
and herself, put them
through good schools and tuba lessons,
taught their kids to play poker

But at the end of the day
she wouldn't lay down

her cards: they had to be pried
from her thin fingers,
spread out before her
till she took their meaning.

She makes me want to dance
dervishly along horizons,
clasp minutes tighter
than tigers clasp prey,
love you now.

The Home's a fine and
(somewhat) private place
but few can find a body
(or a mind) there to embrace.

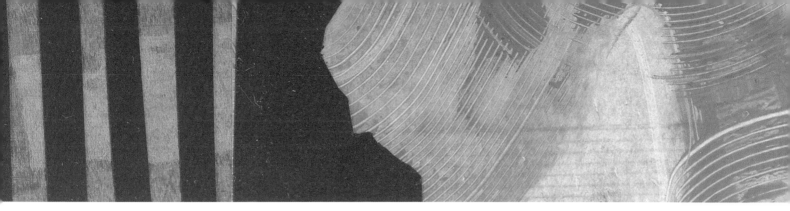

PRISON CELLS

Those who come to live in prison cells are often stunned to find themselves there. In our country today, cells contain those condemned to be executed according to death penalty laws that future generations will look back on as we now look back on legalized slavery. Like South Africa's prisons under apartheid, US prison cells are disproportionately filled with people of color and poor people who don't fit into our economic and political system. Prisons are, for the most part, places of suffering and waste, not obvious signs of the holy.

The word "cell" originated in early Christian monasticism and became part of prison vocabulary when the early Quakers founded penitentiaries as humane alternatives to execution and torture. Like early monks advised by desert ascetics, prisoners were told, "Do not leave your cell. For know by patiently remaining in his cell a monk is led to the ordering of his life." Perhaps the Quakers forgot that free will makes a difference, that persons condemned to prison by others are unlikely to embrace its strictures as a monk who chooses the cell embraces its discipline. Some prisoners, like monks, do repent of their sins, usually in the first few months

Dios
no
mata

of confinement, but as months become years, acceptance often turns to resentment and rage.

Prison cells can become holy places, however, when they lead their inmates to insight, creativity, and resistance. In the Holy Land, I saw the crude holding pen in the ground where Jesus is said to have awaited trial. Who could dare guess at his thoughts while waiting there?

Thomas More's thoughts hallowed the Tower of London while awaiting his execution. He brightened the space with his prayer and witty conversations with his family. There he also wrote, with a piece of coal for a pen, *A Dialogue of Comfort Against Tribulation*, in part to deal with his own fear of likely beheading and disembowelment. In the *Dialogue*, he compares life on earth to a jail, with God as chief jailer of the universal prison, but he concludes with "sure hope in the help of God."

Nelson Mandela set up a school in his Robben Island prison where he helped to train the next generation of South African leaders. He led a campaign to improve prison conditions as part of the struggle against apartheid, where "we fought injustice to preserve our own humanity." For Martin Luther King, the mental anguish of being alone in jail was worse than dying, but again and again he chose to risk going to jail because he believed it led to freedom. He composed his "Letter from a Birmingham Jail" in the margins of newspapers and on the backs of legal papers slipped out of the jail. He wrote primarily to chide local clergymen for their temporizing, but the result is an American classic, a foundational document for the moral and intellectual basis of nonviolent resistance.

Argentinian political prisoner Jacobo Timmerman recalls his feelings of horror and identification when he was thrown into a cell where a previous prisoner had written in blood the extraordinary affirmation "Dios no mata": *God does not kill*. The words gave him hope. Sister Diana Ortiz, raped and tortured in a Guatemalan detention cell, says, "God was with me when I was taken into that building, but my God died in that building." God dies in every prison cell where the divine image in the person is defiled. But God is sometimes reborn in those cells—through the transcendent suffering of their inmates—as stern beauty and improbable grace.

ARREST

They lock us on a bus
reeking of its daily riders,
dirt-swabbed windows
open through the bars.
There are only ten of us,
so we have space and air.

Waiting in the sudden rain
to give our names,
we hold our faces to the wet
before it hits the sweltering cement
and rises again as steam.

In the jail is always day,
or night—whatever it is

when lights are on—and every sound
resounds a thousand times.

We sing camp songs, hymns.
Sharing the too-small floor,
we take turns lying down.
Nobody sleeps. At dawn

they move us to a bigger jail.
Between the buildings, twenty yards
of dew-wet city morning,
camellia petal in the fall.

BORDERS

"Good fences make good neighbors," says the poet Robert Frost, and we do not go beyond his saying. The word "border" conjures up for many, however, not homely but ominous images. The need for some to be on the move because of plague, war, and environmental disaster seems a permanent feature of history, and the daily news carries countless stories of immigrants seeking safety or a livelihood. The Dalai Lama escaping from Tibet, migrant farmworkers dying in the Arizona desert, Edith Stein and millions of other Jews failing to get safe passage to a neutral country during World War II: among the millions facing borders, a few notables get our attention.

Borders have often been drawn against the grain of both nature and culture. Retreating colonialists in Africa and the Middle East drew such borders, which suited themselves and their interests, but by so doing, they sowed a future of violence in those regions.

What if we put our energy into opening up borders instead of delineating, defending, and tightening them?

THE AUCTION

The backgammon board of teak
and the *oud* with inlaid ivory
sell for less than their worth
to these people of modest means.
Now the auctioneer holds up a map.

It is the map of what used to be,
labeled in the language they speak,
their country stolen house by house,
vineyard by bitter vineyard.
The mountains of their hopes

on the flat map abut a salty sea.
The deserts of their longing
surround ancestral towns, fig trees,
olive groves, and cemeteries
where they learned their history.

In the suddenly still room,
the bidding begins at fifty

and climbs—in increments of ten—
to six hundred dollars, by far
the biggest sale this night.

Before the final offer, an old man
and his wife confer. She nods.
In the quiet, no one envies him
as he rises to claim his prize
from the competition all have lost:

the steps to the podium are not
the worn stone threshold of his house
bathed in the fragrance of the jasmine.

Borders also conjure up possibilities. A Hungarian friend of mine walked across three countries with her three children, one of them an infant, during World War II. A vision of freedom kept her mere steps ahead of the invading armies. Others like her receive and rescue treasures across lines of conflict, but peaceful borders better enable an exchange of gifts and cultures.

In his *Crossing Open Ground*, Barry Lopez travels to the tundra where the border between Alaska and Canada "is nearly whimsical." Such a border, invisible for most of its duration, gives "extraordinary release to the imagination." Animals move about undisturbed. No human settlements nor signs of human demarcation meet the eye. Having a foot in two worlds, Lopez loses the desire to see maps. He feels peace and has a difficult re-entry to his home state a few weeks later. There he is asked to vote on zoning, annexation, all determining borders of one kind or another. He feels restive at the need to draw borders, having felt far from them, freed from them for awhile.

Ecologists talk about bioregionalism as a way to save the natural world as well as ourselves. In a bioregional world, communities would be decentralized to live compatibly with natural regions. Maps would be drawn because of watersheds instead of military victories, borders defined by the curving path of a river instead of the linear path of a slide rule. We would work near where we live, eat what is grown there, and live more gently on the earth.

What if we put our energy into opening up borders instead of delineating, defending, and tightening them? What if we let nature rather than conquest draw the lines between us? Could we live more permeably with one another and with nature? Would the earth breathe better and feed our imaginations more richly if we respected trees as fellow beings, if we treated animals like "other nations," as Henry Beston suggests? What gifts might be exchanged with peoples of other races and cultures by opening up borders? What do we lose by failing to cross the border that divides us from our neighbor, which is also the one that divides us from ourselves?

LA MIGRA: SE ATENDIEN PARTOS

"We don't stop pregnant women
at the border," says the INS.

Feeling contractions,
she steps from her house

in Matamoros heat,
catches the local bus to the bridge,
and walks across
to Brownsville.

Showing the border guards
her visitor's pass, she hurries
to another bus and the *partera's*
where her baby gets
what she does not:
a piece of paper with a promise
of school, a vote,
help in old age.

REFUGEE CAMPS

More people seek refuge today than ever in human history. They flee from war, hunger, persecution, and environmental disaster in a vast global movement towards survival. Hungry newcomers erect corrugated tin and cardboard shantytowns on the rims of Third World cities. First World governments erect blocks of flats for those who have abandoned the shantytowns for cities in the North. As rainforests are logged or cleared for oil drilling, indigenous people trek farther into dwindling interiors. In the South Seas, native islands and their peoples drown under rising waters caused by global warming. In the United States, homeless people live under bridges, in parks, in automobiles.

Refugees live at the edges of life. Salvadorans cling precariously to the side of a mountain in Honduras, Sri Lankans sit in a Jordanian desert dazed at their sudden removal from Kuwait, Somalis squat in northeast Kenya hoping for a bit of rice. In camps, refugees collaborate to help make a temporary home for one another. Some organize the children for school and games. Others distribute food. Doctors and nurses give needed shots and

Refugees live at the edges of life.

rehydrate malnourished babies. A community of concern grows up, perhaps a community for prayer. Overcoming the confusion of many languages brings down the Tower of Babel, at least for a few moments, and creates a clear space in the midst of chaos. Extreme conditions give rise to opportunities for patience and compassion.

Throughout the world, refugee camps are places of sanctuary as well as places of desperation. "We have not here a lasting city," proclaims the camp, the tin roof, the corrugated box used for shelter, recalling to us a truth that the solid structures of temples and Houses of Parliament seek to conceal. Tents resemble the dwellings of the Jews on Exodus in the desert. They are "tabernacles," and one was used to house the God of the Jews traversing the desert. This same God reminded the people always to keep sanctuaries, cities of refuge for murderers who had not intended to kill, for aliens in the land, and for those without a place in the current social order. Someone always needs a place of refuge. Someone else can practice compassion by offering it.

God's people have a long history of being refugees. Moses led the Israelites out of Egypt seeking the Promised Land. Jesus, Mary, and Joseph fled from murderous Herod into Egypt. Mohammed, likely to be assassinated in Mecca, took his *hijira* across the desert to Medina, site of the first Muslim community. European Protestants came to America in search of religious freedom. Many Jews escaped from Germany to avoid Hitler's concentration camps, and the Dalai Lama and millions of Tibetans fled Chinese persecution. Every child in a refugee camp is a child of God. Without places of refuge, sanctuaries for sheltering all of God's creatures, the world could not go on.

AL ANDALUS REFUGEE CAMP

I walk between tents lined up like pawns.
My sandals sift sand blown across the
    desert
like those who live here. In the quiet

between moves, a man slumps in the
    shade,
two women carry pails to a pump.

Voices draw me to an open window flap.
Inside, twelve young women wearing
    saris
cluster. Taking turns at a small slice
of mirror, they comb their long black hair.
They could grace a fairy tale,
preening in a sheik's tent.

This is no fantasy: the mirror
rescued from the rifling soldiers
once hung whole in the cellar room
of one who came to work
in a country now at war. Late
at night she combed her hair
and dreamed of home and parents
half a world away. No longer
does the mirror show

the lonely room, its TV, radio,
and other gifts for her trip home.

The strands the women comb
fan out like Indra's net, glow
like candles multiplied by mirrors
in the Jerusalem memorial to children
where a few lights become
the million lost to Holocaust.

Here no candle but the pallid sun
shines through tent flaps.
The mirror captures its light,
captures the women small as children,
captures the first to lose,
 the first to be lost.

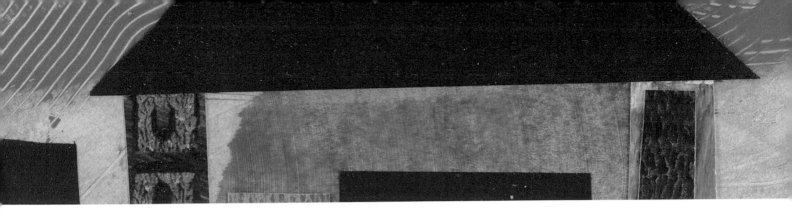

THE HOUSES OF THE POOR

Having visited people living in grass huts in Africa, tents in a Middle Eastern desert, adobe houses, urban flats, and only slightly converted tobacco barns, I've learned that the poorest dwellings foretell both risk and hospitality.

When disaster strikes, poor people sustain the greatest damage. Their houses sit on the low land where the floods sweep in, or on the high land below the coal mine's topped-off mountain that throws down mud and rocks during a storm. In the houses of the poor, children sleep near lead-painted walls, or beside open windows through which the perilous odor of pesticides wafts in from the surrounding fields. Exposed to weather and vulnerable to crime and other violence, their inhabitants must rely on being rather than having.

Empty hands are often open hands, however. An itinerant preacher tells me that the poorest parishes send him away with the most gifts, usually homegrown food and homemade bread. Hospitality, says Henry Nouwen, is creating the space where a stranger can become a friend, and poor households often have the gift of hospitality. I remember a one-room house on a coffee plantation in Honduras.

this shelter will not do

except for
the gardenias and the
curve of solitude

It stood next to a huge concrete slab where millions of gourmet coffee beans lay drying in the sun. The woman we visited there had only a small jar of instant coffee to share—and only one cup for drinking. Four of us spent a lovely afternoon engaged in the ritual of boiling water on an open fire for four cups of coffee, one cup at a time, each one savored in succession, like nectar for the gods.

MONEY ORDER ANGELS

With fingers seamed in sweet potato dirt
the migrant farm workers
count out new hundred dollar bills
for money orders
starchily dispensed
by the clerk

When the winged god
of the US Postal Service
scatters those bills across Mexico,

children have shoes and notebooks for
    school
beans and a chicken on Sunday
Grandmother gets new teeth
and wives smile at husband memories

Like an Advent Angel
announcing that this birth counts
that someone can be counted on
the money orders fly
on filaments of faith
to brighten
barest rooms

We live in a time of shelter magazines and TV shows. Entire sections of the newspaper focus on the renovation and decoration of our homes. Malls feature stores selling accessories for the upscale household. These publications and stores do not target people with little disposable income, the ones more likely to live lightly on the earth. Those who

use up less of the earth's resources seem to under-
stand that in many languages "home" means family,
not the piling up of artifacts and gadgets.

   Living at risk and living in a spirit of hospitality
are both signs of the presence of God. Both require
that we depend on someone or something outside
and beyond us. We cannot save ourselves, and we
don't share out of superabundance. We share be-
cause we recognize our own neediness. Of ourselves,
we may not have the energy or the resources to take
in the stranger, but God will provide, we hope, we
pray. The Psalmist prays to live in the house of God
and asks God, again and again, to be shelter. Where
shelter is an image for God and the doors remain
open, home can become a holy place.

      An unpainted
      shack in the bend of a sandy track
      through scrub pines choked by kudzu

      Two gardenia
      bushes taller than the rusty roof
      astonishing both sight and smell

In winter
a wood fire bleats through chinks
where slaves once stared into the dark

In summer
stove heat chases to the porch
an aproned woman with Nefertiti's nose

Unlike the red
brick singles, sheet-rocked for comfort,
along the straight paved road

Like lean-to's
in the Yucatan and thatched huts
everywhere, this shelter will not do

Except for
the gardenias and the curve of solitude
looping the pines on the arc of the world

THE STREETS OF THE POOR

Hundreds of millions of human beings live in ghettos, barrios, shantytowns, urban neighborhoods, and rural villages. Visitors to India from the West universally remark how everything—birth, death, cooking, family life—takes place on the streets. In most cultures, the upper classes have greater access to privacy. Their courtyards, balconies, and porticos shelter their private lives. The meanest streets showcase human desperation, but courage, even joy, can thrive there too.

In her autobiography, *The Long Loneliness*, Dorothy Day recalls the outdoor coffee line at the Catholic Worker in New York during the Depression. She laments that the men have no coats, some lack underwear, and their feet show through the cracks in their shoes. She confesses to a lack of patience with a few who drink, but she admires most for their endurance and "the hope which they cling to in the face of tremendous odds."

Outside a homeless shelter in the city near me, men stand on the street early in the morning waiting for trucks to come by and pick them up for day labor. A few slouch singly against the wall, but others stand out at the curb, talking and joking,

hopeful that the day will bring some work, that an employer will choose them. It occurs to me that the ones with hope are more likely to be chosen.

A friend of mine describes morning and evening on the streets of Nairobi when tens of thousands, mostly men, who can't afford even the price of a crowded *matatu*, or minibus, walk ten or fifteen miles either going to a job or looking for a job. They walk quietly, many of them gaunt and ill shod, but they have a camaradarie among themselves and talk freely to those who walk along with them. I think of the millions who wait and walk like this when I hear a farmworker union organizer in the United States say, "We have no money, but we do have time—that's all we have—and we will prevail."

In the neighborhoods of poor people, a spirit of community often cohabits with the deprivation. Dorothy Day speaks of visiting Harrisburg in the 1940s, where "the night was alive with dark faces and bodies, sitting on the steps of the ramshackle houses, nursing their babies, watching their children, listening to the music, the rhythm of tambou-rines, the clapping of hands, the singing from the Tabernacles, churches of the Lord, the Pentecostal churches on every corner." Lest her rendition sound romantic, she also mentions "the smell of rats, the smell of dead things, the smell of rotting garbage. If you have ever been in a town where there are stock-yards, fertilizer factories, paper mills, you know the peculiar odors of our industrial system. They are not sweet."

In 1989, when people were still coping with a war and the aftermath of a virulent earthquake in El Salvador, I visited a barrio of squatters in the capital who had partially rebuilt their houses from the rubble of toppled buildings. The government had run some wires nearby that were intended to carry electricity to another, more middle-class neighborhood. The barrio residents knew they couldn't get away with it for long, but they tapped into the electricity for a few hours in order to have a party. Shared food, dancing, and games for the children celebrated their sense of possibility despite the human and natural forces arrayed against them.

It was for only one day, but it was a day they would not soon forget.

TEGUCIGALPA CALLE

Old woman with thin feet
    thin dress
    drawn face
heavy basket of golden
flowers on your head:

I remember the bakery in Granada,
a slim breeze on a sun-pressed day,
a facsimile of a strawberry soda
and a little girl on the stool beside me
      eating cake
      finishing a coke
then staring at my empty glass.

Then I saw
her bloated belly
    narrow jaws
    glassy eyes,
this scavenger of Coca-Colas.

To McDonald's here in Teguc
she comes too
begging first for coins
picking pieces of potato chips
    from the benches
rooting in the garbage bin
until the clean-up man
who could be her father
chases her with emphasis.
She does not laugh but screams
in the game of death
and hangs at the door
mocking his endurance.

How do I drink my coffee,
        eat my ice cream
in face of this?
        Because there are so many:
were one child hungry,
I could feed it;
were it only today,
I could sustain it.
        But feed just one
and ten more take its place,
take one home
and thousands more go unregarded.

Old woman with thin feet
that walk where your daughters'
daughters are hungry:
how can we bring them flowers?
how can we bring them bread?

THE ARTIST'S SPACE

Holy places are those where beauty struggles to be born.

Artists may wait on inspiration, but carrying dreams to completion demands that they be utterly materialistic. The stuff for bringing vision to reality includes paint, paper, wood, brushes, easels, mallets, knives, concrete, and metal. Artists have to find places for working and storing and vehicles for hauling.

One sculptor friend of mine jammed on her brakes and pulled to the side of the road wherever and whenever she saw a fallen tree. She had to measure it then and there in case it might serve for a work she had in mind. Some of her acquaintances thought her otherworldly, but the men at the foundry where she took her pieces to be bronzed knew her as "the gutsy lady" in overalls with muscles like the rest of them.

In an artist's studio, the material of earth is transformed by the sweat and muscle and vision of the artist into a new dimension of the real. The artist's attention to the task is a prayer, a contemplative work—sometimes performed in chaos, sometimes in calm—that opens onto truth and invites us to at-

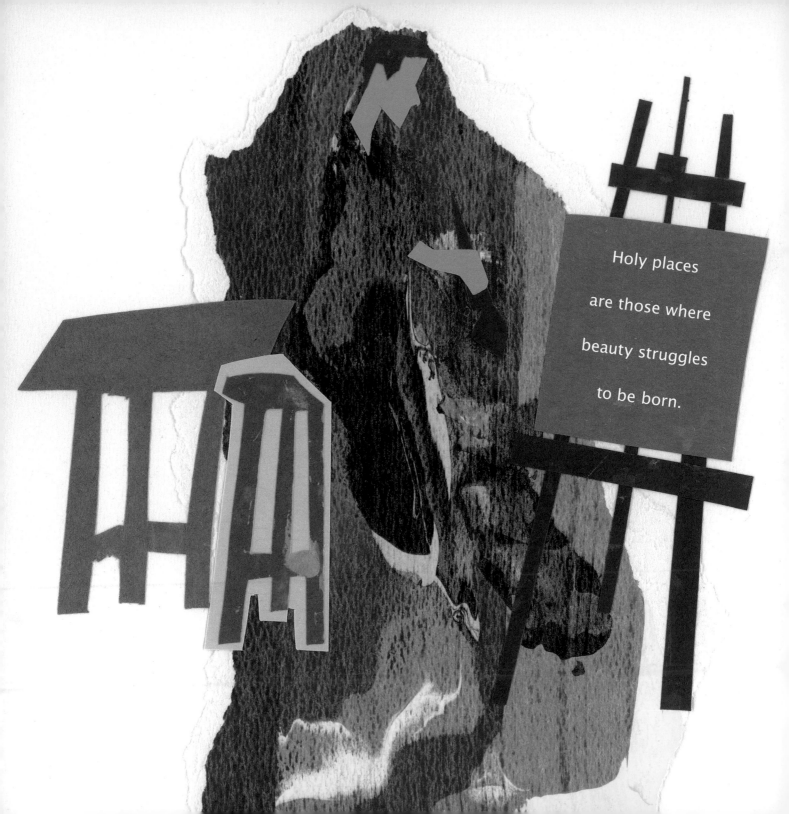

Holy places

are those where

beauty struggles

to be born.

tend to it as well. The artist's passion births a beauty that compels our attention but allows us to admire without needing to possess. "We want to eat all the other objects of desire," says philosopher Simone Weil. "The beautiful is that which we desire without wishing to eat it. We desire that it should be."

Artists can work in solitude, or they can—like actors, directors, and musical conductors—create community in their artistic spaces, each space a clearing for contemplating a myriad of human perspectives. Helen David Brancato believes the creative person can transform any space into an energized atmosphere for the artistic process. No matter how small the room, it can become a sacred space for contemplation, incubation, and action. "I am most energized," she says, "when I am with others who are also engaged in 'doing and making,' who are then willing to talk about the process." Her communal studio at the Southwest Community Art Center in Philadelphia can't contain all the energy bouncing off its walls. "In this sacred, joyous space, people nourish each other's spirits. We buoy one another in times of worry and sorrow, and our need for each other is evident and reflected in the work."

"In the midst of this atmosphere," Helen continues, "I can also get so lost in my own reflective process that I am lifted to another level of consciousness or meditation—totally unaware of time or what is going on around me. Recently I was given a large studio space for four months. My initial reaction was loneliness because I have been so used to being surrounded by my creative friends at the Center. My question to myself is, 'Can my spirit transform this studio into a holy, energized space?' We'll see."

Simone Weil thinks that "contact with the beautiful is a sacrament in the full sense of the word." Beauty is one incarnation of God in the world, and experiencing beauty, a sign of the presence of God. It follows that all great art, no matter its content, in essence is religious. In 1995, the Philadelphia Museum of Art mounted a remarkable exhibit of Constantine Brancusi's sculptures that seemed to illustrate this truth. The exhibit inhabited a vast white space that emulated the sculptor's own

Paris studio. The white helped him focus on the timelessness of what he was creating.

Brancusi wished to reduce his forms to essential elements that could evoke the purest emotions. He used natural materials, highly polished wood and stone and metal, carved and honed into curves and spheres, quintessential birds and fish and human beings. One of his favorite subjects was the Maiastra, a legendary Romanian bird with marvelous song and feathers. Many of his arrangements seem trinitarian, communitarian. Life stands on tiptoe, emergent, essential but in flux. Most of the pieces are heavy but seem light as air, utterly graceful. Visitors to the exhibit felt themselves walking in a sacred space. It captured, in Brancusi's own words, "pure joy."

BRANCUSI AT THE PHILADELPHIA MUSEUM OF ART

I.

Is all prayer this dark figure
bending over a grave? Torment,
a fevered child?
Two kissing,
one slab of life?

Subtracting for bird
fish muse child
gives us more, who roam
the galleries
and suspend grief

when children whisper
"E.T." or "See the giant
ant." Ovoids fill up
voided hearts, mines,
dark holes and dreams.

II.

"I give you pure joy," he said, a flock
of birds easing into the empyrean
blue bronze white black
and full cups of oak,
holes in the head of Socrates
(his ears and mouth? What did
they hear in Athens? Did he say?),
cocks that comb the air
and slice an egg, waking
children's faces muses
Prometheus the world.

Our stiff hands curl
to cup this life stuff,
cradle the morning spheres, the
    newborn
emergent in the mouth's line, nose's
mere ridge, curve of the eye
like a butterfly's wing.

III.

One stainless steel sphere
reflects like crystal
three penguins: a Holy Family,
nuns in an embrace,
the Trinity.

Maiastra that becomes a plumped
gold bird becomes a weighty
weightless bird in space.
A slim fish swims
in air, a flat and yellow paddle hand
rocking no boat.

Like the giant cups, we
scoop up the joy. The cock
corrugates our plane lives.
Eye and mouth lines
marry etchings on the soul,
a key unlocking light.

Our stiff hands curl
to cup this life stuff,
cradle the morning spheres, the
newborn
emergent in the mouth's line, nose's
mere ridge, curve
of the eye
like a butterfly's wing.

IV.

    What flight
expect from these birds,
this flying turtle round as Turtle Island,
this cock of pinking shears that cuts
the wind, the guts
inside the dawn?

As wood absorbs the light,
metal mirrors it,
and marble veined like flesh
remembers how
at our setting out
golden Leda put on shape divine
and suffered through the birth of beauty,
ultimate sculptor of earth.

WORKS CITED

Brancusi, Constantin. *Constantin Brancusi Retrospective.* Philadelphia Museum of Art, 1995.

Chaucer, Geoffrey. *The Canterbury Tales.* Translated by Neville Coghill. Baltimore, MD: Penguin, 1952.

Day, Dorothy. *The Long Loneliness.* New York: Harper, 1952.

Frost, Robert. "Mending Wall," in *North of Boston.* London: David Null, 1914.

Hammarskjöld, Dag. *Markings.* Translated by Leif Sjöberg and W.H. Auden. London: Faber and Faber, 1964; New York: Knopf, 1964. Originally published in Swedish as *Vägmärken.* Stockholm: Bonniers, 1963.

Herbert, George (1633). "The Temple" in *George Herbert: The Country Parson, The Temple.* Edited by John N. Wall, Jr. Mahwah, N.J.: Paulist Press, 1981.

King, Martin Luther. "Letter from a Birmingham Jail." April 16, 1963, Birmingham, Alabama, in *Why We Can't Wait.* Edited by Martin Luther King, Jr.   www.kingpapers.org

Lopez, Barry. *Crossing Open Ground.* New York: Vintage Books, 1989.

Marley, Bob. "Zion Train."

Merton, Thomas. *Day of a Stranger.* Salt Lake City, Utah: Gibbs M. Smith, 1981.

More, Thomas. "A Dialogue of Comfort Against Tribulation," in *The Yale Edition of the Complete Works of Saint Thomas More.* New Haven: Yale University Press, 1963.

McGovern, Robert. *The Door to the Road Taken.* Woodcut.

Thoreau, Henry David. *Walden, or: Life in the Woods.* Boston: Ticknor and Fields, 1854.

da Viterbo, Ilaria. *L'Annunciazione (The Annunciation).* Porciuncula Chapel, Assisi, Italy. Painting, 1393 (circa).

THOUGHTS FOR CONTEMPLATION
& DISCUSSION

1. Can your life be told in terms of place? What places hold the greatest meaning for you?

2. In-between spaces are venues for possibility. Think about the in-between spaces in your life. Where were you coming from? Where were you going? What possibilities were birthed there?

3. "Holy places are those where beauty struggles to be born." What unlikely "holy places" have you experienced?

4. Many contemplatives choose to live amid "urban madness." Why do you imagine this is so?

5. Sailboats are womb-like vessels, bearing within them life that is ever evolving and ever changing. What are some other "womb-like" spaces you've spent time in? What makes places like this different from other sacred spaces?

6. "What if we put our energy into opening up borders instead of delineating, defending, and tightening them?" How might the world be transformed if world governments began to take steps in this direction—for better and for worse?

7. Are there any soulless, spiritless places in your life? What steps might you take to transform and sanctify these spaces?

8. Have you ever offered another in need a sacred space? Have you ever been offered sacred space? What did the offering or the receiving of such a gift mean to you?

AFTERWORD

. . . they say that her soul left Rome
and stopped at a friend's in Siena
to prepare a meal
before she, happily ever after,
burst into God.

—Evelyn Mattern, from "Catherine of Siena"
in *Why Not Become Fire?*

Evelyn's passionate desire to write about sacred spaces and thresholds was perhaps a premonition of her death. Nearing the end of her life, Evelyn told her close friend and frequent collaborator, Helen David Brancato, "I'm not here nor there—I'm in the in-between."

Evelyn burst into God on November 30, 2003 after a short bout with cancer.

WALKING SOFTLY THROUGH SACRED SPACES

In remembrance of the life of Evelyn Mattern
by Evelyn's niece, Jennifer Mattern

The theme of sacred spaces was one that my aunt held dear, a theme that revealed itself time and time again in her words, both spoken and written. I share this abridged version of the eulogy I wrote for Evelyn's memorial service in the hope that it might better illuminate her remarkable life, "a life told in terms of place," a life spent seeking—and bearing witness to—the sacred in the ordinary. Always.

My aunt, Evelyn Mattern, once heard Zen master Katagiri Roshi speak. She was deeply moved by one of his phrases in particular: *the silence of trees exactly*. On her last visit to our home before she died, she said to me, "I'm not sure what it meant, but it stuck with me."

It stuck with me, too, and I found myself thinking of this phrase on the evening that she died. *The silence of trees exactly*. The world indeed seemed more silent, more still than usual that night.

I remember Evelyn, speaking so passionately at my wedding of the trees of the mythical Forest of Arden. She was an impressive scholar of Shake-speare, and she was especially enamored of the play *As You Like It*. When Evelyn officiated at our outdoor wedding celebration in 2000 (and she did indeed "officiate," running the show like a magnificent high priestess) my usually soft-spoken aunt surprised everyone by flinging her arms wide and proclaiming with great gusto to the trees and the congregation alike: "Today we are here to witness a comedy!"

A comedy! This was no ordinary wedding. But this was no ordinary preacher, either. Having captured everyone's attention with her opening line, she continued:

"We are here to witness a comedy. I'm talking about something very like a Shakespearean comedy, one that takes place in a 'green world,' to which many persons have come from various noisy and even threatening locales. 'So this is the Forest of Arden,' says Rosalind, the heroine of *As You Like It*. The characters have fled to the Forest as Jennifer and David have come to the country here to delight in its serenity . . . And we who are here tonight with them also immerse ourselves in the natural rhythms of life so easily forgotten in the city."

I think of Evelyn's beloved cabin, the place she referred to as Peace Hill, nestled in a "green world" perhaps not unlike the Forest of Arden. My aunt was, among many things, a lover of trees. There exists a wonderful bit of home movie footage, circa 1973 or 1974, of my aunt lying on her back beneath the dogwood tree in front of my childhood home, picking blossoms and tucking them into her hair while my brother and I played nearby. And, when she visited us for the first time at our Massachusetts home, the first thing she did was to lead our barefoot, newly walking daughter into our backyard, to point out the different types of evergreens to her—trees that we ourselves had taken for granted.

The silence of trees exactly. It occurs to me that the silence of trees is a fleeting thing. Stand in a silent wood or in a quiet grove of trees, and you know without a doubt—*expect*, even—that it will only be a matter of moments before another breeze sails through to set the leaves rustling once again. The silence of trees is never a permanent state. And I cannot help but think that this stillness, this quiet that has settled upon us with the news of her passing, is a temporary state as well. The wind has let up for a moment in the Forest of Arden, that's all.

I want to tell you that we, too, are witnessing a comedy. In Evelyn's words: "Traditional Shakespearean comedy begins in confusion. Characters lose track of one another in the woods, they see fairies and sprites, they hide behind trees and hear what they shouldn't. They always mistake appearance for reality."

I will dare to tell you this: I believe that we, the supporting cast of characters, have simply lost track of our beloved heroine in the woods. I like to think she is hiding behind the next tree over, just out of sight, eavesdropping on us. Let us not mistake the absence of her tangible presence as reality. The genuine, authentic reality is this: in Shakespeare as in life, the comic heroine never dies.

During her life's work she bore witness to a great deal of pain and suffering. She bore witness to profound tragedy, almost daily, in the forgotten places of this world—ghettos, barrios, killing fields, refugee camps. She chose to use her life to serve the castaways, the castoffs—migrant farmworkers, death-row inmates, Iraqi women and children, the poor of our country and abroad. And yet, my aunt was loath to cast anyone she worked with as a tragic figure. I think she sensed that doing so would invoke pity instead of inviting action. And Evelyn was all about action.

And here is what I have always found remarkable about my aunt's particular brand of action: when there was no more to be done, when battles had been fought and lost, she continued to act by bearing witness to the injustice she saw in this world. She bore witness by writing and speaking and praying and breaking bread with the lost—and by refusing to turn away from the many who were crying out to be seen and to be heard.

One article written about Evelyn described her as "a tree standing tall in the face of injustice." This is an apt statement, but there was more, so much more. I would tell anyone who asked—and those who did not think to—that her glass was not just half full, but fairly brimming with hope and gratitude, and with laughter unearthed in the most unexpected of places. I would tell them that Evelyn's world was as lush and green and vibrant as the Forest of Arden, and just as wonderfully unpredictable.

Today, the magical Forest of Arden is silent, and we are uncomfortable in its stillness. The loss of her physical presence has rendered us tongue-tied. What can be said of such an extraordinary person,

such a remarkable spirit? The words come too fast, or not at all.

But by gathering here today, we echo her life. We bear witness to a life of witness. And soon, the wind will return to the forest, and we will hear her again, in the leaves rustling overhead. We will see her again, in the work of others, in the work of each other. Keep an eye out, and you may just catch a glimpse of her, popping her head out from behind a favorite tree.

Our heroine is not so far away; she is only a few trees ahead. So let the comedy continue. In Shakespeare's words, from *As You Like It*, words that my aunt also shared at our wedding:

> *There is mirth in heaven*
> *When earthly things made even*
> *Atone together*

Evelyn, you will surely have little to atone for. And now that you are there, there is even more mirth in heaven. Lucky them. And lucky us, to have played a part in your comedy. We'll meet you on the other side of the forest.

—J.M.

ABOUT THE AUTHOR & ILLUSTRATOR

Evelyn Mattern (author, *right*) was a well-known peace activist, writer, teacher, and world traveler. The acclaimed author of *Why Not Become Fire?* and *Blessed Are You: The Beatitudes and Our Survival* (Ave Maria Press), Mattern was once described as "a gentle burr in the side of the rich and powerful, and a comfort and confidante to the powerless." Mattern and collaborator Brancato led numerous contemplative workshops together, incorporating guided sessions in writing, art, and meditation. Although Mattern passed away in late 2003 after a battle with cancer, her writings reflect her passionate, unwavering belief in a world where justice, peace, and environmental advocacy are the norm rather than the exception.

Helen David Brancato (illustrator, *left*) is an accomplished painter and art educator as well as a longtime collaborator with Evelyn Mattern. Brancato's illustrations have appeared in numerous books and magazines, including Henri Nouwen's *Walk with Jesus: Stations of the Cross* (Orbis Books) and *Maryknoll*. She is an adjunct professor of painting and drawing at Villanova University in Philadelphia.